PEOPLES of NORTH AMERICA

Nez Perce

VALERIE BODDEN

CREATIVE EDUCATION • CREATIVE PAPERBACKS

Published by Creative Education and Creative Paperbacks
P.O. Box 227, Mankato, Minnesota 56002
Creative Education and Creative Paperbacks
are imprints of The Creative Company
www.thecreativecompany.us

Design and production by Christine Vanderbeek
Art direction by Rita Marshall
Printed in Malaysia

Photographs by Alamy (Arco Images GmbH, Everett Collection Historical, Everett Collection Inc,
Historic Collection, Niday Picture Library, Robert Harding Picture Library Ltd, nik wheeler),
Corbis (167/Drew Rush/Ocean, Blue Lantern Studio, Bohemian Nomad Picturemakers, Corbis,
Macduff Everton, Connie Ricca, Joseph Sohm/Visions of America, Nik Wheeler, Marilyn
Angel Wynn/Nativestock Pictures), Getty Images (Stock Montage), iStockphoto (foofie), Library
of Congress, Shutterstock (fivespots, Ronnie Howard, Gregory Johnston, Pete Niesen,
OHishiapply, Sylvana Rega, Tom Reichner, Transia Design, worldswildlifewonders)

Library of Congress Cataloging-in-Publication Data
Bodden, Valerie.
Nez Perce / Valerie Bodden.
p. cm. — (Peoples of North America) • Includes bibliographical references and index.
Summary: A history of the people and events that influenced the North American Indian tribe
known as the Nez Perce, including Chief Joseph and conflicts such as the Battle of the Big Hole.
ISBN 978-1-60818-554-2 (hardcover)
ISBN 978-1-62832-155-5 (pbk)
1. Nez Percé Indians—History—Juvenile literature. 2. Nez Percé Indians—
Social life and customs—Juvenile literature. I. Title.

E99.N5B63 2015
979.5004'974124—dc23   2014041749

CCSS: RI.5.1, 2, 3, 5, 6, 8, 9; RH.6-8.4, 5, 6, 7, 8, 9

First Edition HC 9 8 7 6 5 4 3 2 1
First Edition PBK 9 8 7 6 5 4 3 2 1

PEOPLES of NORTH AMERICA

Nez Perce

VALERIE BODDEN

CREATIVE EDUCATION • CREATIVE PAPERBACKS

Table of Contents

❖⊶⊷⊶ Non-treaty Nez Perce of the 1870s (on page 3);
horseback-riding Nez Perce (pictured here) ⊶⊷⊶❖

Introduction

For thousands of years, the Nez Perce Indians ranged over the Columbia **PLATEAU** in what is now the northwestern United States. Their homeland stretched from the Bitterroot Mountains in the east to the Blue Mountains in the west. In between was nearly every landscape imaginable: Grasses, flowers, and edible plants bowed in the breeze on the high, flat prairies, while sagebrush and rabbitbrush poked up from the floors of deep, desert-like canyons. Gentle, rolling hills carpeted by grasses gave way to high mountain slopes tangled with pine, fir, and hemlock. Deer, elk, and pronghorn roamed the land, and **SPAWNING** salmon fought their way upstream through clear, cold rivers churning with mountain snowmelt. The Nez Perce traveled through this country on foot and, later, horseback, moving with the seasons to reap the natural bounty.

The Nez Perce called themselves *Nimiipuu*, meaning "The People" or "The Real People." French traders named them "Nez Perce" for "pierced nose." Perhaps they either saw some Nez Perce wearing nose piercings or misinterpreted the tribe's name in the Indian sign language. In addition to a new name, Europeans brought a new culture to the Nez Perce—one that some accepted and others rejected. Those who rejected it eventually found themselves at odds with the U.S. Army. After the fighting subsided, divisions between the groups remained, and today the Nez Perce live on two separate reservations. But at both, the people continue to celebrate aspects of their traditional culture.

BETWEEN THE BLUE MOUNTAINS AND SNAKE RIVER ARE THE WALLOWA MOUNTAINS OF OREGON.

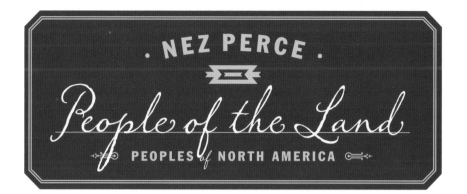

NEZ PERCE

People of the Land

PEOPLES of NORTH AMERICA

ANTHROPOLOGISTS believe that the ancestors of the Nez Perce settled in the Columbia Plateau around 10,000 years ago. At first, the population was likely small, but it grew until the Nez Perce occupied a region covering parts of present-day Oregon, Washington, and Idaho. The ancestral Nez Perce likely speared large game, gathered mussels and wild plants, and fished. The earliest Nez Perce ancestors may have lived in caves and holes in the canyon walls or set up camp in the open. But around 4,500 years ago, they began to build pit houses. These were shelters with floors dug a few feet into the ground. The part of the shelter that was above ground was probably made of poles covered with brush or bark.

Later, the Nez Perce built large communal lodges in place of pit houses. These structures were made of two walls that angled in toward each other, forming a triangle. The walls were covered with mats woven from cattail stalks, reeds, or grasses. Sometimes the floor was dug into the ground. A lodge could be 100 feet (30.5 m) or longer and house up to 30 families. Everyone slept along the walls of the lodge, and each family built its own fire in the center of the structure. The smoke went up through openings at the top of the lodge.

The Nez Perce lived in their lodges during the winter, when they settled

IDAHO LAKES AND FORESTS MADE GOOD FISHING
AND HUNTING GROUNDS FOR THE ANCESTORS OF
THE NEZ PERCE.

into villages in the canyons. There they were protected from the worst of the snow and cold. Most villages were set up along streams, where the Nez Perce could find fish and firewood. By about 1700, the Nez Perce lived in 70 to 130 villages throughout their homeland. A few villages contained up to 300 people. But the majority generally included anywhere from 30 to 100 members, most of whom belonged to an extended family group. In addition to one or more lodges, a village usually also included dome-shaped huts for sweat baths and other ceremonies, as well as an area for holding ritual dances.

In the spring, villagers left their lodges to travel to fishing, hunting, and gathering camps. Instead of building new lodges at each camp, they usually set up cone-shaped tepees. The walls of the earliest tepees were covered with mats made of bark or reeds, but these materials were later replaced by bison hides.

The Nez Perce spoke a language belonging to the Sahaptin language family. The languages of many other tribes on the Columbia Plateau—including the Cayuse, Molala, Palouse, Tenino, Umatilla, Walla Walla, and Yakama—were closely related. Other Plateau tribes, such as the Spokan, spoke unrelated languages. Many Nez Perce learned the languages of their neighbors. In addition, most of the tribes used a common sign language to communicate with one another.

The Columbia Plateau was home to more than 20 different Indian peoples, but by 1700, the Nez Perce were the most influential. For the most part, the Plateau tribes got along well. Many of the groups observed a similar culture or freely adopted aspects of one another's. The Nez Perce intermarried with many other Plateau tribes, especially the Palouse and Cayuse. In addition, they

FEAST OF FISH *Fish made up about half of the average Nez Perce's diet. Each year, Nez Perce fishermen pulled 2 to 3 million pounds (907,185–1.4 million kg) of fish—mostly salmon—from the area's rivers. That allowed each individual to eat up to 500 pounds (227 kg) of fish annually—more than a pound (0.5 kg) a day. In addition to serving as an important food source, salmon were considered sacred, as was the water in which they swam.*

often traveled to fish, hunt, or visit among neighboring tribes. Members of other tribes came to Nez Perce villages to take part in feasts and ceremonies. A few Nez Perce traveled as far as the Great Plains to hunt.

Among the major reasons the Indian tribes got together was for trade. They exchanged not only goods they had made themselves but also items they had obtained through trade with other tribes. Goods from the Pacific coast, the Great Plains, Mexico, and Canada all made their way to the Plateau. The Nez Perce provided bows, salmon oil, baskets, and other goods for trade.

In the 1730s, trade with the Shoshone brought the Nez Perce their first horses. Soon, the Nez Perce had become avid horsemen, with a herd numbering in the thousands. Many Nez Perce practiced selective breeding, developing horses that were long-legged and sure-footed, known for their endurance and speed. Nez Perce horses were in demand from the Northwest to the Great Plains, and they reached not only other Indian tribes but also American and European traders. According to one trader, Nez Perce horses were "fit to mount a prince." In addition to trading the animals, many Nez Perce kept hundreds of horses for themselves. A large

⤝ FIERCE FIGHTERS ⤞ *Even as they fought the Nez Perce, American soldiers admired their opponents' bravery. The Indians charged into battle on their horses "in regular daredevil style," according to Sergeant Michael McCarthy. Another officer described their tactics: "They ride up behind little elevations, throw themselves from their ponies, fire, and are off like rockets." Or they crawled across the ground with grass tied to their heads, "so that it is hard to tell which bunch of grass does not conceal an Indian with a ... rifle."*

herd became a symbol of wealth and power.

Nez Perce riders controlled their horses with only a thin strip of bison **SINEW**, and those who watched them astride their animals admired how the Indians appeared to be "grown to their backs." Horses made travel easier. The Nez Perce could load supplies and goods for trade onto the horses to reach distant trade and hunting grounds. With horses, the Nez Perce ranged farther west to acquire dried shellfish, baskets, wooden tools, and seashells. Travel extended to the east as well, as large family groups crossed the Bitterroot Mountains to hunt bison on the Great Plains.

Sometimes these hunting parties remained on the Plains for up to two years. There they lived and hunted with Plains tribes such as the Flathead, Crow, and Kutenai and traded with others such as the Eastern Shoshone. Through these exchanges, the Nez Perce adopted the use of hide-covered tepees, **TRAVOIS**, and eagle-feather war bonnets. They incorporated Plains songs and dances into their ceremonies.

Not all Nez Perce adopted the Plains lifestyle. Those living farthest east, near the Bitterroot Mountains and the Clearwater River, traveled to the Plains most frequently. They came to be

THOUGH THEY DO
NOT LIVE AS FAR
SOUTH ALONG THE
SNAKE (ABOVE),
TODAY'S NEZ
PERCE ARE STILL
ROOTED IN THE
HOMELAND.

known as the Upper Nez Perce. Those who lived farther south and west, near the Salmon and Snake rivers, traveled less frequently, and they became known as the Lower Nez Perce. The two groups may have spoken slightly different **DIALECTS** of the Nez Perce language, since they were so separated from one another.

Both the Upper and the Lower Nez Perce sometimes came into conflict with other Indian groups, even those with whom they had trade relationships. On the Plains, the Nez Perce sometimes fought with the Blackfeet, who also raided the Nez Perce homeland. To the north, the Nez Perce did battle with the Spokan or the Coeur d'Alene. But their most feared enemies came from the south: the Shoshone, the Paiute, and, especially, the Bannock, who often raided Nez Perce villages. The Nez Perce retaliated with raids of their own, from which they sometimes brought back captives to serve as slaves.

The Nez Perce fought hard to defend their land because they believed it was part of their identity. The land provided them with food such as fish, game, and wild berries and roots. The mountains that surrounded them offered protection from outsiders. But above all, the Nez Perce felt deeply connected to the land. That connection was reflected in a common saying: "I am of this land."

A lthough the Nez Perce shared a common culture and language, they did not consider themselves to be a unified group under one leader. Instead, each Nez Perce village was led by its own headman. A headman was usually the village's most respected older man. His job included serving as the village's spokesman and helping to resolve villagers' disputes.

The position of headman was generally hereditary, although a headman could be replaced if he proved to be ineffective. The village headman was chosen and advised by a council made up of the male heads of each family in the village. The council advised the headman concerning village issues, fishing and hunting plans, and relations with other groups. Both the headman and the council ruled by **CONSENSUS**. They could not require people to follow their decisions. If a person did not agree with them, he was free to ignore them or to move to another village.

Although each village was independent, several neighboring villages might join together to form a band. The various villages of the band usually came together to fish, harvest wild plants, hold ceremonies, and defend their territory from attacks by outsiders. Bands were led by their own council, made up of representatives from each village. The band council chose a leader,

Each Nez Perce family member knew his or her role in keeping the tight-knit villages running smoothly.

THE APPALOOSA
HORSES SPECIALLY
BRED BY THE NEZ
PERCE WERE SCAT-
TERED THROUGH-
OUT THE WEST BY
THE 1900S.

usually known as a band headman or chief. Like the position of village headman, that of band chief was hereditary. It usually went to the headman of the band's largest village. As with village leaders, the band council and chief ruled by consensus.

At times, neighboring bands joined together to form larger groups known as composite bands. These groups sometimes traveled to the Great Plains to hunt. Or they came together to gather foods, conduct ceremonies, or fight against enemies. As in villages and bands, the composite band was led by a headman and a council who ruled by consensus.

Most villages, bands, and composite bands also added the position of war chief to their leadership at some point in their history. The war chief led the group in times of war or on large hunts. Like the headman, the war chief was chosen by the council. In some cases, the same person served as both headman and war chief.

Although warfare had always been part of the Nez Perce way of life, it took on a larger role once the Nez Perce made contact with tribes from the Plains. The Nez Perce adopted many of the war customs of the Plains peoples, including raiding for horses, rewarding warriors with war honors, and holding war dances. Nez Perce warriors also imitated the Plains practice of "counting coup," in which they tried to get close enough to touch an enemy warrior and escape alive. Nez Perce warriors rode into battle on horseback, carrying bows made from sheep horn and, later, guns. Although the Nez Perce had saddles, warriors generally rode into battle bareback or atop only a small saddle blanket.

When they weren't at war, the daily life of the Nez Perce

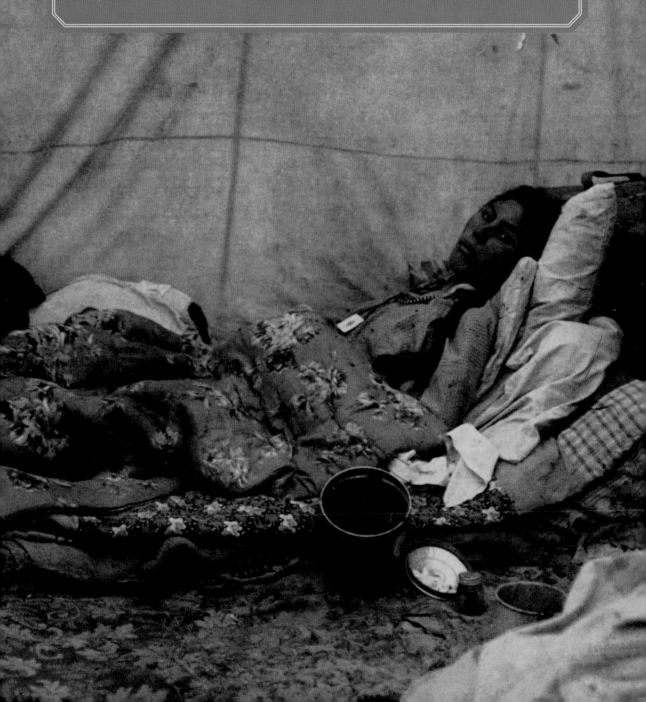

Being Nez Perce

⇢─☞ **DEFENSELESS AGAINST DISEASE** ☜─⇠ *When European explorers arrived in the Americas, they brought with them a host of new diseases. Since the Indians had never been exposed to such diseases before, their bodies had no defense against them. In 1781, a smallpox epidemic wiped out nearly half of the Nez Perce population. Then, in 1847, outbreaks of measles reached the Plateau tribes. Rumors flew that the diseases had been intentionally introduced by missionaries or that missionaries were handing out poison instead of medicine. Such rumors sometimes led to violence.*

changed with the seasons and revolved around obtaining food. In the spring, men hunted rabbits and waterfowl, first strapping on snowshoes if there was still snow on the ground. Women collected the season's earliest roots, which grew along the streams near their villages.

In late May and early June, the villagers traveled to their favorite fishing sites to get ready for the year's first run of salmon. Soon the rivers were clogged with fish swimming upstream from the Pacific Ocean to reach their spawning grounds. At the best fishing locations, the Nez Perce maintained fishing stations, where they constructed weirs, or fences, of brush to trap the fish. At some stations, they built wooden platforms over the rushing waters of the river from which they could net or spear the fish. Some fishermen also used **HARPOONS**, **SEINES**, or hooks and lines.

Their main catch was salmon, but the Nez Perce also took sturgeon, whitefish, and trout. Some of the fish was eaten immediately—either raw or cooked on a stick over a fire. The rest was dried and stored in underground **CACHES** for winter.

After the spring salmon run, Nez Perce bands generally set up camps at higher elevations. There the women gathered wild roots and plants such as camas (whose bulbs tasted like sweet potatoes), serviceberries, blackberries, and sunflower seeds. As with fish, some of the plants were eaten immediately, while others were prepared and stored for winter use.

In the fall, the Nez Perce concentrated on supplementing their winter stores. The women continued to collect plants, and another large run of fish was caught and stored. Fall was also the best time for hunting big game such as deer, elk, moose, and mountain sheep and goats. Carrying bows and arrows as well as spears, hunters waited for their prey at **SALT LICKS** and watering places or stalked them through the forest. Sometimes they disguised

A TRADITIONAL METHOD OF GRILLING SALMON INVOLVED STAKING THE FILLETED FISH INTO THE GROUND ENCIRCLING A FIRE.

themselves in animal skins and antlers to creep up on the animals. Or a group of hunters might form a circle around an animal and close in to trap and kill it.

In October or November, the Nez Perce returned to their villages. They spent the cold winter days making clothing and tools. Children listened as the elders recounted Nez Perce legends that taught important lessons.

Throughout the year, Nez Perce children were generally raised by their grandparents. Aunts and uncles played a role in training them as well. By the time they were three or four years old, girls learned to dig up roots, and boys were given small bows and arrows with which to practice future skills.

When boys and girls were around nine years old, they went on a vision quest. For a vision quest, a child was left in the wilderness without food or water for several days and nights. He hoped to have a vision of a *wyakin*, or guardian spirit, who would help and protect him. A guardian spirit could be an animal, a natural

Being Nez Perce

⇢⇢ **"DO THEM NO HURT"** ⇠⇠ *When Meriwether Lewis and William Clark first reached the Nez Perce, some wanted to kill the newcomers. But others argued that the Americans might provide them with new, powerful weapons. Then an elderly woman named Returned spoke up. She had once been captured by the Blackfeet and then sold to a white man before making her way home. Whites had been kind to her and helped her, she said. "Do them no hurt." The Nez Perce heeded her advice.*

occurrence (such as lightning), or a supernatural being. Each person's guardian spirit was thought to provide special powers. A deer, for example, brought swiftness, and a grizzly bear meant strength in battle. If a child did not see a vision, it was taken as a sign that he or she would have a difficult life. But the child could choose to go on another vision quest in hope of receiving a guardian spirit.

Throughout their lives, the Nez Perce continued to call on their guardian spirits, and they learned how to please their spirits with the help of a *tewat*, or **SHAMAN**. Both men and women could serve as shamans, and those who took on this role were believed to have a special ability to communicate with spirits. In addition to teaching people how to understand their guardian spirits, shamans led ceremonies, foretold the future, and acted as healers.

LEWIS AND CLARK USED THE NEZ PERCE'S LOLO TRAIL TO CROSS THE BITTERROOTS ON THEIR WESTWARD AND EASTWARD TRIPS.

From Contact to Conflict

PEOPLES *of* NORTH AMERICA

The first European explorers arrived in the Americas in the late 1400s, but they did not reach the lands of the Nez Perce for nearly 300 years. Even before their first contact with Europeans, though, the Nez Perce had learned of the newcomers through interaction with other tribes. They had obtained European items—most notably horses—through trade with other Indian peoples and had encountered guns in the hands of their enemies, the Blackfeet.

In 1805, the first U.S. citizens entered the Nez Perce homeland. They were part of the Corps of Discovery, an expedition led by Meriwether Lewis and William Clark to explore the American Northwest. The Nez Perce provided the explorers with food, and the Corps remained with them for two and a half weeks before continuing on to the Pacific.

The next spring, the Corps returned eastward and spent several weeks with the Nez Perce. The two groups got along well, and when Lewis and Clark told the Indians about the powerful American government, the Nez Perce promised to "always give [the Americans] every assistance in their power." When Lewis and Clark left the Nez Perce, they estimated the tribe's population to be around 6,000.

LEWIS AND CLARK WERE GRATEFUL FOR THE NEZ PERCE'S HOSPITALITY—AND THE HORSES OBTAINED THROUGH TRADE.

Within five years of Lewis and Clark's visit, trappers and traders had made their way to the Northwest, spurred by the explorers' reports of abundant beavers and other fur-bearing animals. The Nez Perce provided the traders with horses, food, clothing, and bison robes. In return, they received guns and ammunition, knives, tobacco, and manufactured goods.

In 1836, the first missionaries set up a church in the Nez Perce homeland. They were well received by many Nez Perce. But others resented the missionaries' attempts to change their culture and force them to adopt American-style clothing, learn English, and become farmers. Soon, the tribe was divided between those who had adopted the "road of the whites" and those who chose to retain their traditional practices.

The Nez Perce were led farther along the "road of the whites" in 1842, when the American government demanded they select a single "high chief of the tribe." The headmen chose a minor chief named Ellis for this role, but they likely considered him simply a spokesman for their people, with no real authority over the bands, which retained their headmen. The Americans, however, intended for the head chief to have the authority to negotiate on behalf of all Nez Perce.

In 1855, the Nez Perce and other Plateau tribes were called to a council with the governor of Washington Territory, Isaac Ingalls Stevens. Stevens wanted the Indians' lands for settlers and for the construction of a railroad. He ordered the tribes to move onto reservations. The Nez Perce reservation was to be largely on the tribe's traditional homeland, although they would have to give up some of their hunting and grazing grounds. Most Nez Perce headmen at first rejected the treaty. They said that the earth could not

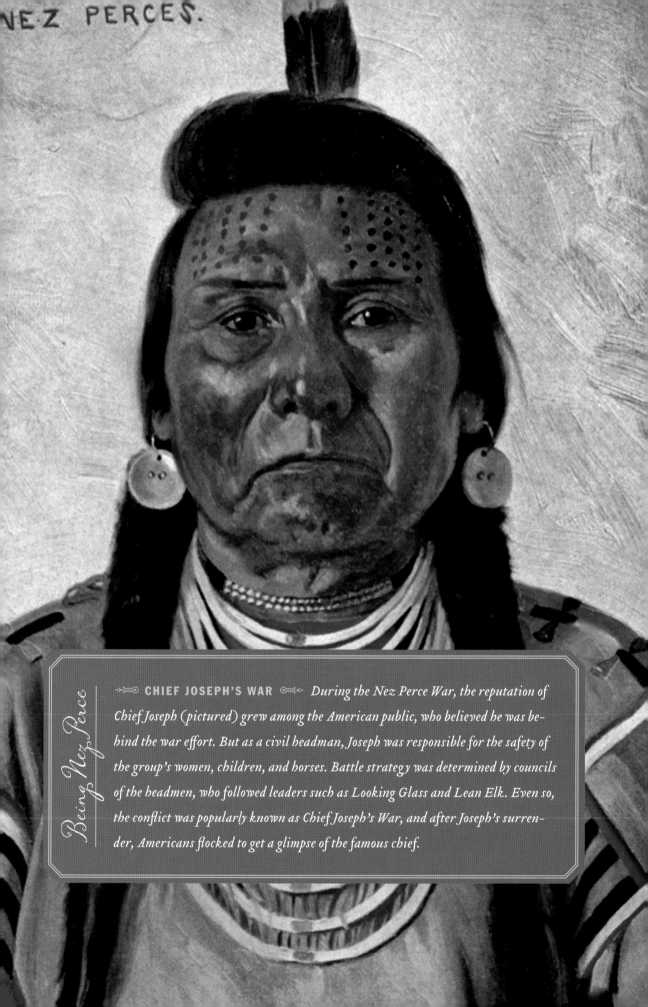

NEZ PERCES.

➤━══ CHIEF JOSEPH'S WAR ══━☜ ➤ *During the Nez Perce War, the reputation of Chief Joseph (pictured) grew among the American public, who believed he was behind the war effort. But as a civil headman, Joseph was responsible for the safety of the group's women, children, and horses. Battle strategy was determined by councils of the headmen, who followed leaders such as Looking Glass and Lean Elk. Even so, the conflict was popularly known as Chief Joseph's War, and after Joseph's surrender, Americans flocked to get a glimpse of the famous chief.*

be bought and sold. But Stevens convinced the new Nez Perce head chief, named Lawyer, that a treaty was the best way to remain at peace with the powerful American government. Ultimately, Lawyer helped persuade all the headmen to sign the document.

Less than a month after the treaty was signed, settlers began to move onto the lands that had been ceded by the Nez Perce and other Plateau tribes. Almost immediately, warfare broke out between the settlers and many of the Indians. Although the Nez Perce remained peaceful, some settlers hanged a Nez Perce man. By 1856, many of the Nez Perce headmen—including Old Joseph, the headman of the Nez Perce band in northeastern Oregon's Wallowa Valley—had had enough. They wanted to dissolve the 1855 treaty. Lawyer and others insisted, however, that the entire tribe was bound by the terms of the treaty. Those who continued to support the 1855 treaty became known as the Treaties. Those who opposed it were known as the Non-treaties.

Although the 1855 treaty was supposed to keep Americans off the Nez Perce reservation, in October 1860, prospectors discovered gold on the reservation's northern edges. By 1862, nearly 19,000 whites had moved onto the reservation to prospect illegally. Entire

⟜◦⟞ BATTLE OF THE BIG HOLE ⟝◦⟜ *On August 8, 1877, the fleeing Non-treaty Nez Perce camped in a wide, grassy valley in Montana known as the Big Hole. They thought they were far ahead of their American pursuers. And they were. But that night, a separate American force from Montana crept into position around the camp. Early the next morning, they opened fire, shooting low into the tepees to hit the sleeping Indians. Although the Nez Perce fought back, 60 to 90 were killed, most of them women and children.*

cities, such as present-day Lewiston, Idaho, sprang up as the prospectors built wagon roads, hotels, saloons, stores, and houses. The Treaty Nez Perce did not object to the white presence on the reservation. In fact, many profited from it by serving as guides or selling supplies and livestock to the miners. The Non-treaties, however, were angered by the white presence and threatened war. By 1862, the situation was so tense that the miners began to call on the government to remove the Indians from the reservation.

The government obliged. In June 1863, the Nez Perce were asked to sign a new treaty giving up almost 7 million acres (2.8 million ha)—nearly 90 percent of the land that had been guaranteed to them in the 1855 treaty. The lands of the Treaty Nez Perce would not be affected, and they were willing to sign the new agreement. But several Non-treaty bands, including those led by Old Joseph, White Bird, and Toohulhulsote, would be required to give up their homelands and move onto the new, smaller reservation. They refused. On the night of June 4, all the Nez Perce headmen gathered. When they couldn't come to an agreement, the Non-treaties, "in an emotional manner, declared the Nez Perce nation *dissolved*," according to an American observer. As leaders

from the two sides shook hands, the Non-treaties told Lawyer and his followers that "they would be friends, but a distinct people." With that, the Non-treaties left the council.

Despite the division of the tribe, government officials pressured the remaining headmen to sign the treaty. Eventually, they did so. Even though none of the headmen who signed the treaty represented the bands whose land was given up, the government considered the treaty binding for all Nez Perce.

The Non-treaty bands refused to move. By 1871, their lands were beginning to fill with white settlers. That year, Old Joseph died. His son, Young Joseph (or Joseph the Younger), who became known as Chief Joseph, took his place as headman and continued to fight for his people's land. "Neither Lawyer nor any other chief had authority to sell this land," he said. "It has always belonged to my people." Government officials who reviewed the 1863 treaty decided that Joseph was right. In 1873, the government set aside part of the Wallowa Valley for Joseph's band. But after a public outcry (among settlers), the decision was reversed, and Chief Joseph's people were again told to move.

In May 1877, Joseph and the other Non-treaty bands were given an ultimatum: they could move onto the reservation peacefully—or they would forcibly be taken there by American soldiers. Fearing for the safety of their women and children, the headmen agreed to move. They were given 30 days.

NEZ PERCE

War and Exile

PEOPLES of NORTH AMERICA

Before they moved onto the reservation, the Non-treaties gathered one last time at a favorite camping spot called Split Rocks. Their group numbered around 200 warriors and 400 women, children, and old men, along with some 3,000 horses. On June 13 or 14, only days before the deadline to move onto the reservation, a small group of young warriors rode out of the camp. Over the next three days, they vented their anger by killing more than a dozen white settlers. Although the killings had not been ordered by Non-treaty leaders, they knew the army would retaliate. They instructed their people to move to a safer location in White Bird Canyon.

There the warriors readied themselves for an army attack, which came on June 17. Although only about 50 to 70 Nez Perce fighters had weapons—mostly bows and arrows and outdated guns—they forced the American army of 100-some men to retreat. The Nez Perce gathered up the weapons of the fallen soldiers. Then they fled across the Salmon River with their families and horses. They were soon joined by additional fleeing families, bringing their total number to about 750. Altogether, the group had only 250 warriors.

Over the course of the next 3 and a half months, the Nez Perce traveled more than 1,500 miles (2,414 km) across present-day Oregon, Idaho,

AFTER HE FLED THE LAPWAI RESERVATION,
LOOKING GLASS JOINED CHIEF JOSEPH AND
LED THE RESISTERS TO BIG HOLE.

THE SITE OF CHIEF JOSEPH'S SUR- RENDER AT BEAR PAW BATTLEFIELD IS THE LAST STOP ALONG THE NEZ PERCE NATIONAL HISTORIC TRAIL.

Wyoming, and Montana, with various army units in constant pursuit. Although the army caught up with them on several occasions and the two sides engaged in frequent battles, the Nez Perce were always able to escape.

At first, the Nez Perce headed for the Great Plains, where they hoped to find safety among the Crow Indians. But when they reached Crow territory in September 1877, they learned that their longtime hunting partners had sided with the Americans. Now the Nez Perce's only hope was to flee to Canada.

On September 29, 1877, the Nez Perce stopped to rest near the Bear Paw Mountains, less than 40 miles (64.4 km) from the Canadian border. The next morning, 400 American troops launched a surprise attack on the camp. After a five-day **SIEGE**, during which some of the Nez Perce managed to escape toward Canada, Chief Joseph finally agreed to surrender on October 5. "I am tired of fighting," he said. "My heart is sick and sad. From where the sun now stands, I will fight no more forever."

During the war, approximately 100 to 200 Nez Perce had been killed—many of them women and children. Those who surrendered were taken to Fort Leavenworth, Kansas. There they froze through a harsh winter and then roasted during a hot and humid summer that brought mosquitoes carrying **MALARIA**. Many died.

In July 1878, the Nez Perce were again moved, this time to Indian Territory in present-day Oklahoma, where they continued to suffer from the heat and disease. They were joined by many Nez Perce who had returned from Canada only to be captured by U.S. troops. Chief Joseph pleaded with American officials to

➤ ➤ **JUST SAY NO TO MINING** ➤ ➤ *In 2005, mining corporations requested the right to mine Mount Tolman on the Colville Reservation. The mountain was a rich source of an element called molybdenum (muh-LIB-dih-num), which is used in steel, fertilizer, and dyes. The companies promised the reservation would see profits of up to $1 billion from the mines and an influx of 400 jobs. Although the reservation needed the money, voters rejected the proposal. Mount Tolman was a sacred prayer site, and many also worried about the pollution a mine would cause.*

allow his people to return to their homeland. In January 1879, he traveled to Washington, D.C., where he addressed a large crowd of American and foreign officials. "You might as well expect all rivers to run backward as that any man who was born a free man should be contented penned up and denied liberty," he told them. "We only ask an even chance to live as other men live."

Despite Joseph's plea, in June 1879, the Nez Perce were moved to a new location in Indian Territory. Most lived in tepees covered by rotten canvas. Children and old people died in large numbers, and doctors reported a 100 percent death rate among newborns.

Finally in May 1883, 29 Nez Perce women, children, and old men were allowed to return to the Nez Perce reservation at Lapwai, Idaho. Two years later, the rest of the Nez Perce in Indian Territory left, too. Of the nearly 500 Nez Perce who had been sent there, only 268 had survived. Because officials feared that Americans in Idaho would seek revenge on the Indians, fewer than half of the survivors were allowed to resettle on the reservation there. The rest—including Chief Joseph—were sent to the Colville Reservation in Washington. The new reservation was home to several different Indian tribes, some of them unfriendly toward the Nez Perce.

On the Colville Reservation, most Nez Perce chose to live in tepees, collect wild plants, and hunt. But on the reservation at Lapwai, divisions remained between the Christians and the non-Christians. In general, the non-Christians followed a traditional lifestyle, while the Christians lived in American-style houses, wore American-style clothing, farmed, and sent their children to school to learn English.

In 1887, the Nez Perce reservations were broken into **ALLOTMENTS**, and each Nez Perce individual received a section of land. Any remaining land was opened to white settlers. By 1910, the

IN THE EARLY 1900S, COLVILLE RESERVATION MEMBERS WERE PHOTOGRAPHED IN CLOTHING MORE TYPICAL OF PLAINS TRIBES.

AS THE NEZ
PERCE LOOK TO
RESTORE NATURAL
BALANCE IN THEIR
HOMELAND, THEY
PASS ALONG RITU-
ALS TO THE NEXT
GENERATION.

Idaho reservation was home to 30,000 whites, who lived among the scattered allotments of the 1,500 Nez Perce there. Towns soon sprang up as well, along with public schools attended by both white and Nez Perce children. The Nez Perce culture slowly faded.

When the U.S. entered World War II in 1941, many Nez Perce served in the armed forces. Others left the reservation to work in the defense industry. Although some never returned to the reservation, others went back to form a new tribal government, which worked to improve education, housing, health, and sanitation on the reservation.

In the 1990s, tribal efforts were directed toward improving environmental conditions. Nez Perce scientists worked to reintroduce salmon to rivers where they had almost died out as dams prevented them from swimming upstream to spawn. The Nez Perce were also instrumental in reintroducing wolves—which had disappeared from the West in the 1930s—to their homeland.

NEZ PERCE NATIONAL HISTORICAL PARK *Today, visitors to the Columbia Plateau region can tour Nez Perce National Historical Park, which covers 38 different sites of significance to the Nez Perce. The Nez Perce National Historic Trail connects many of these places and follows the path of the Nez Perce flight from the U.S. Army in 1877. Extending from Wallowa Lake in northeastern Oregon through Idaho and Wyoming to the Bear Paw Battlefield in Montana where Chief Joseph surrendered, the trail covers 1,170 miles (1,883 km).*

Today, about 3,500 people belong to the Nez Perce tribe. Approximately 2,700 of them live on the Nez Perce Reservation in Idaho, while others continue to live on the Colville Reservation or in cities off the reservation. On both reservations, many Nez Perce have worked to revive their traditional culture. Some continue to speak their native language, and many still hunt and gather wild plants. Every year, the Nez Perce hold powwows, where they remember their past through songs and dances.

The Nez Perce know that honoring the past helps to ensure their future. It is a way of "maintaining ... the knowledge that made this land a wonderful place to live," according to Nez Perce Taz E. E. Conner. Life for the Nez Perce has changed much in their 10,000-year history. From their early days living in pit houses and hunting big game to their first encounters with outside explorers and warfare, the Nez Perce have faced many challenges. Although those trials have at times divided them, the Nez Perce today are united in their determination to preserve their traditions and culture.

LOCAL HISTORY IS CELEBRATED BY RESIDENTS OF ALL BACKGROUNDS DURING CHIEF JOSEPH DAYS IN JOSEPH, OREGON.

The Nez Perce passed the long winters listening to stories told to them by the tribe's elders. The stories taught lessons and helped to explain the world around the Nez Perce. Many tales featured animals with human traits. A favorite character was Coyote. In this story, Coyote saves the animals from a monster and then creates the first humans.

Long ago, the world was filled with animals. But a huge monster ate them all. When Coyote learned of this, he approached the monster. He told the monster that it might as well swallow him, too, since all the other animals were gone and he didn't want to be lonely. So the monster took a deep, gulping breath and sucked Coyote into his mouth. Coyote walked down the monster's throat, where he saw the bones of many animals. As Coyote traveled toward the monster's heart, a bear rushed out and growled at him. Coyote kicked the bear in the nose. That is why all bears now have flat noses. Then a rattlesnake shook its tail at Coyote, and Coyote kicked it in the head. Now all rattlesnakes have flat heads. As he got closer to the monster's heart, Coyote told the animals to pick up some wood. When he reached the heart, Coyote used the wood to start a fire. Soon, smoke was pouring from the monster. The monster wanted to kick Coyote out, but Coyote talked the monster into letting him stay.

By now, the monster was thrashing in pain. Coyote grabbed a stone knife and began cutting the monster's heart. When his knife broke, he took out another knife and began cutting again. That knife broke, too, but Coyote had three more. As each knife broke, Coyote told the animals to get ready to flee. Then, after his last knife broke, Coyote jumped onto the heart and pulled it loose. The monster died, and the animals escaped. Muskrat lagged behind and made it out just in time, but his tail was trapped, and the hair was pulled off it—and it remains bare today.

As they made their escape, the animals carried the bones of the dead animals from inside the monster. Coyote sprinkled the monster's blood on the bones, and they came back to life. Then Coyote cut up the monster's body. He threw pieces of it across the land. Wherever they landed, a different people sprang up: the Blackfeet, Cayuse, and others. When Coyote had thrown the last piece, Fox turned to him and asked, "But who will live here?" Then Coyote washed the blood of the monster from his hands and sprinkled it on the land where he stood. And from that blood came the Nimiipuu. They were smaller than the other peoples around them, but Coyote promised they would be powerful. Coyote left the heart of the monster as a large, rocky mound in their land— and it is still there today.

ALLOTMENTS
portions set aside for individuals; many American Indians were forced to take allotments from tribal lands, with any remaining lands going to the U.S. government

ANTHROPOLOGISTS
people who study the physical traits, cultures, and relationships of different peoples

CACHES
hidden storage areas for food or other supplies

CONSENSUS
agreement by all or most of a group

DIALECTS
forms of a language that use specific pronunciations, grammar, or vocabularies that differ from other forms of the language; speakers of different dialects of the same language can usually understand each other

HARPOONS
fishing tools consisting of a spear attached to a rope

MALARIA
a disease that causes chills, fever, and often death and is spread to humans by mosquitoes

PLATEAU
a high, flat expanse of land

SALT LICKS
natural deposits of salt on the ground that animals lick

SEINES
long fishing nets that hang vertically in the water, with floats on the top and weights on the bottom

SHAMAN
a spiritual leader often believed to have healing and other powers

SIEGE
a military attack in which an army surrounds the enemy to force a surrender

SINEW
a tendon, or cord, that connects muscle to bone

SPAWNING
depositing eggs into water

TRAVOIS
a vehicle made of two poles crossed into a V-shape at one end, with a bison hide hung between them to serve as a platform; the travois was hitched to a dog or horse, with the ends dragging on the ground

Cassidy, James, ed. *Through Indian Eyes: The Untold Story of Native American Peoples.* Pleasantville, N.Y.: Reader's Digest, 1995.

Hampton, Bruce. *Children of Grace: The Nez Perce War of 1877.* New York: Henry Holt, 1994.

Josephy, Alvin M. Jr. *500 Nations: An Illustrated History of North American Indians.* New York: Knopf, 1994.

———. *Nez Perce Country.* Lincoln: University of Nebraska, 2007.

Kehoe, Alice B. *North American Indians: A Comprehensive Account.* 2nd ed. Englewood Cliffs, N.J.: Prentice Hall, 1992.

Philip, Neil. *The Great Circle: A History of the First Nations.* New York: Clarion, 2006.

Schofield, Brian. *Selling Your Father's Bones: America's 140-Year War against the Nez Perce Tribe.* New York: Simon & Schuster, 2009.

West, Elliott. *The Last Indian War: The Nez Perce Story.* New York: Oxford University Press, 2009.

╺⊷ READ MORE ⊶╸

Dwyer, Helen, ed. *Peoples of the Southwest, West, and North.* Redding, Conn.: Brown Bear, 2009.

King, David C. *The Nez Perce.* New York: Marshall Cavendish Benchmark, 2008.

╺⊷ WEBSITES ⊶╸

LANDSCAPE OF HISTORY: THE NEZ PERCE (NEE-ME-POO) NATIONAL HISTORIC TRAIL
https://www.youtube.com /watch?v=PMEVav1Mixw&feature=youtu.be
Get a glimpse of the Nez Perce flight from U.S. troops in this official U.S. Forest Service video.

NEZ PERCE NATIONAL HISTORICAL PARK: MUSEUM COLLECTIONS
http://www.nps.gov/museum/exhibits/nepe /index.html
Learn more about Nez Perce life and check out pictures of Nez Perce artifacts.

NOTE: EVERY EFFORT HAS BEEN MADE TO ENSURE THAT THE WEBSITES LISTED ABOVE ARE SUITABLE FOR CHILDREN, THAT THEY HAVE EDUCATIONAL VALUE, AND THAT THEY CONTAIN NO INAPPROPRIATE MATERIAL. HOWEVER, BECAUSE OF THE NATURE OF THE INTERNET, IT IS IMPOSSIBLE TO GUARANTEE THAT THESE SITES WILL REMAIN ACTIVE INDEFINITELY OR THAT THEIR CONTENTS WILL NOT BE ALTERED.